AF449899

Mummy Papa Chachu Chachi

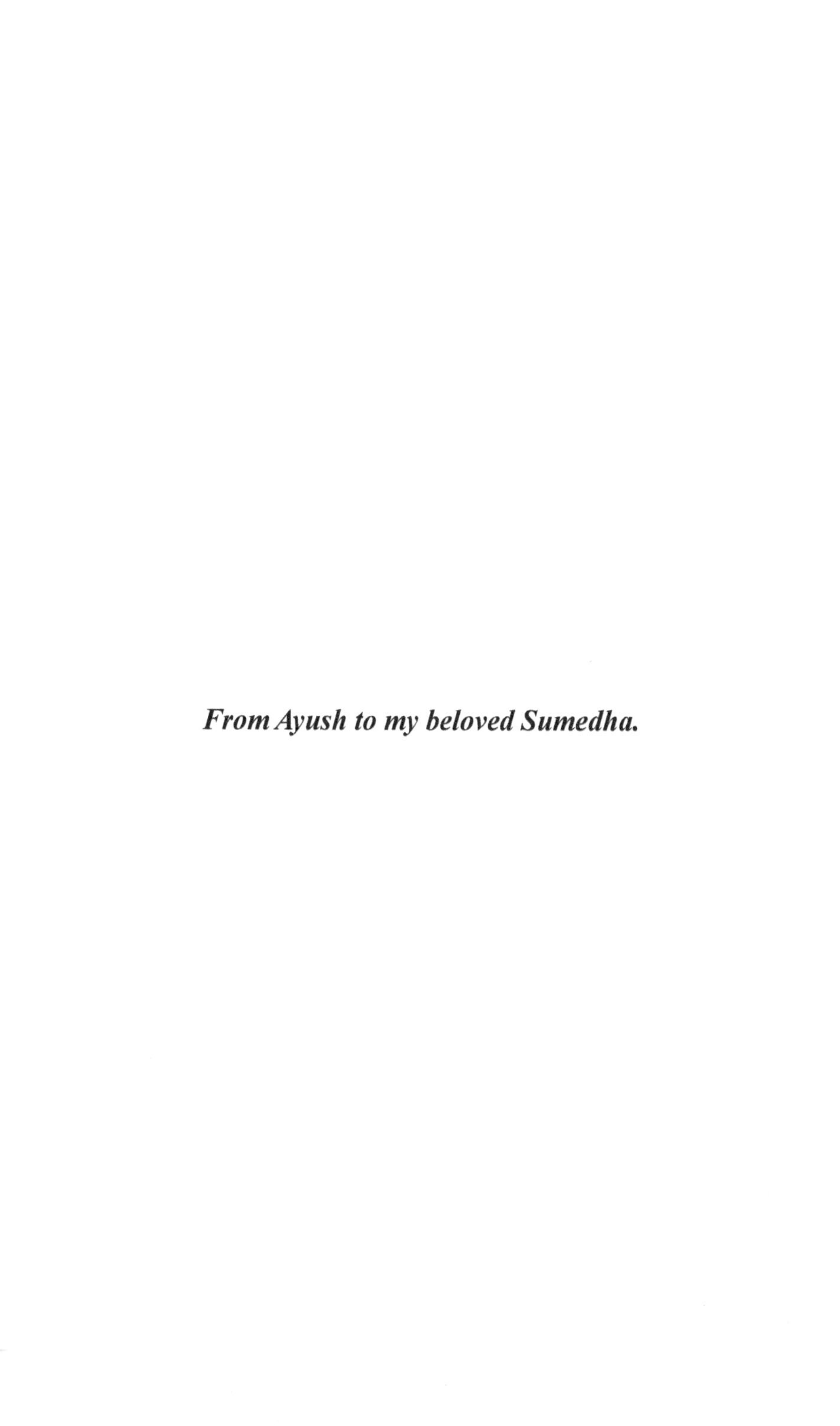

From Ayush to my beloved Sumedha.

ELECTION ON MARS

Ayush Garodia

Contents

Prologue – 1- 2

I – Lift Off – 3 - 5

II – A Foreign Land – 6 - 11

III – Chaos – 12 - 15

IV – Home? – 16 - 24

V – Final Speech – 25 - 31

VI – 1 – 32 - 42

VII – 2 – 43 - 50

VIII – Regret – 51 - 55

IX – Phobos – 56 - 64

X – Election Day – 65 - 75

Prologue

Humans: we are all so different, so unique in our own ways. Each person lives a different life in a world of their own. But when you widen the lens and view from another part of the universe, it's just us as a whole—humanity, a life found only on Earth and soon on other planets. Humanity has come so far by breaking itself into numerous parts, with each part contributing to its advancement, much like the human body.

Through collective consciousness of millions of years, of the dead and alive, humanity has grown, akin to the roots of a tree, with each generation deepening its existence. One way to help this process has been governance. The idea is excellent—a small group with the responsibility to aid the rest, ultimately expanding our collective existence.

The concept of governance has continuously evolved, but there's something intrinsic about it. With great power comes great responsibility, yet for great responsibility, great power must also be given. The process of bestowing this power and finding the right individuals to exercise it has always been challenging. Many forms of transferring power have come and gone, from inheriting power and fighting wars for it to the current system where democracy reigns supreme and competent leaders are chosen by the people. But is the power held by these leaders justifiable? In this ever-changing world, is it still acceptable to adhere to the same ideologies of governance developed centuries ago?

Implementing change in our current world is challenging, but what about Mars? A new planet free from all earthly norms. As we humans eye new settlements on Mars, seeking to form colonies, trying to expand human consciousness in this expanding universe, is it finally the time to also change the way humanity governs itself?

Could it finally be time for a change?

I

It was late at night. The city had slept. Far away from the coastline, the world laid shrouded in darkness, a vast expanse of water extending endlessly into the distance. The silence was deafening, broken only by the gentle, rhythmic clapping of the waves against an unseen shore. Amidst the stillness, a glimmer of light flickered into existence. Filled with life, it was ready to explore the depths of true darkness. The people aboard the ship felt a sense of unease as they prepared to embark on this unprecedented journey. Among them sat a young man, his mind racing with unanswered questions, his only companion being a small white-furred creature beside him.

His mind was blank but was recalling a memory of a lifetime. He had no idea why he was on that damn thing. Questions kept piling up with no answers in sight. He tried to get up from his seat, but the restraints held him down firmly. He felt as if he were trapped in a surreal reality and had nowhere to go. Taking a break from his intrusive thoughts, he leaned towards his furry friend and tried to grasp its paw, but the seat belts did not allow him to. There he sat, a prisoner in his seat, facing the infinite.

His heart raced inside his suit, as if it was trying to escape his chest. Memories he had buried long ago resurfaced in his mind, draining him of all hope. He closed his eyes, but the darkness that greeted him only amplified his fears. His suit felt like a device designed specifically for his demise. The countdown was at T-100 and he still could not comprehend why he was in that godforsaken contraption.

Countless reasons swirled in his mind, yet not one made any sense.

He asked himself, "Why am I doing this? Why am I trying to retrieve something I lost long ago? Have I lost my mind?"

The only response he received was silence.

He could feel like he was drowning in the storm of his own thoughts.

The sky was a clear expanse above him, but his anxious breath clouded his vision. With the countdown at T-50, he realized he had no escape from the inevitable. With one final, desperate gasp for air, he closed his eyes.

In that moment, his mind wandered back when the same announcement was made. He felt the same rush of emotions that had consumed him, seven years ago. He saw the young boy he once was, sitting in the crowd, eyes wide with wonder and fear. Just a few miles away, watching it all and knowing he could do nothing about it. The memory was vivid and visceral, as if he were living it all over again.

As T-10 approached, a tear escaped his eye, and not a single question had been answered.

The countdown reached zero. The engines ignited and began to rumble beneath him. The entire cabin started shaking violently and the young man could feel the intense vibrations coursing through his body. He was pressed back into his seat with a force that threatened to crush him.

He closed his eyes. His mind was empty. Despite the chaos around, a sense of calm settled over him. Perhaps, he was exactly where he was meant to be. Perhaps all the answers he sought were waiting for him on the other side.

Dissecting the sky, the beam of light left for Mars.

II

After months of traversing through space, the rocket finally touched down at Martian base. The tension inside the cramped cabin was tangible as the passengers waited for the chambers to open. With a hiss, the airlock doors slid open, and a troupe of humanoid robots emerged. They promptly attended to the passengers, meticulously verifying that each suit was suitable for the journey ahead.

The young man was greeted by one of the robots. Its voice carried a strikingly human-like warmth.

"How was your trip, sir?" the robot inquired, its optic sensors locking onto the man with a compelling intensity.

He couldn't suppress a smile at the robot's polite inquiry, though a flicker of uncertainty danced behind his eyes. "I didn't expect it to be so comfortable," he replied, his voice betraying a hint of awe. "The journey was truly unforgettable."

He pivoted, scanning the faces of his fellow travellers,

everyone suited up and ready to embark. The robots guided the passengers out of the cramped confines of the rocket, into the unknown vastness of Mars. As the young man stepped onto the crimson soil, he felt a shiver run down his spine as his boots made contact with the foreign terrain.

He took a few moments to look around, absorbing the sights and sounds of this new world. Despite feeling light in his suit, he managed to walk alongside the other passengers. Together with his companion, he entered the rocket station for further medical screenings. As they made their way through the corridors of the station, each step felt to him like a deliberate movement through the fabric of reality.

The medical screening concluded, and the young man and his companion headed to the embassy situated within the rocket station to finalize paperwork. To their astonishment, the embassy had organized a cab to transport them to their destination. The cab whisked the duo away to the nearest hotel, Hotel Red Planet.

As they stepped into the hotel's cavernous lobby, the young man's eyes widened with wonder at the sheer size of the place. Long, winding corridors stretched out before them. Just then, they were greeted by another robot.

"Welcome to the Red Planet, the grandest hotel on Mars," the robot intoned, its voice carrying a melodic cadence.

"Thank you," replied the young man. "We're here to check in."

"Can you show me your ticket so I can check you into your room?" the robot asked.

The young man promptly showed his and his companion's tickets to the robot, and it quickly processed their information.

"Hello, Mr. Shiba and Marco Jr.," the robot said. "Would you prefer a room with a view of the city?"

"Yes, that would be perfect," he replied.

The receptionist helped Shiba and Marco find a room offering a panoramic view of Mars. Finally, after what felt like an eternity of wearing their space suits, they could relieve themselves from the weight of the cumbersome attire. They settled in, Shiba ordered some food for him and Marco and put their space suit on charge. After a satisfying meal, he fell into a deep sleep, trying to recover from the long journey.

The next day, Shiba woke up with a restless energy pulsating through him. He sprung out of his bed and decided to explore the planet by taking an air tour.

Hovering above the cityscape, Shiba found himself amazed by the unique architecture of Mars. Every building was shaped like an egg, and the large oval structures stood out like a sore thumb against the red, rocky landscape. The city unfolded before him, it was unlike any city he had ever witnessed. Vibrant colours danced across the surrounding rocks and valleys, a captivating contrast against the butterscotch skies overhead. Surprisingly, the streets below remained uncluttered, devoid of the typical traffic he was accustomed to.

Following the tour, Shiba returned to his room, and fed Marco. Sitting by the window, he was enjoying the panoramic view of the planet before him when his phone suddenly rang.

Answering the call, Shiba was greeted by a familiar voice on the other end. "Welcome to Mars," the voice intoned.

Caught off guard, Shiba's face turned pale. "How do you know I've arrived?" he inquired, his voice barely audible.

The other voice chuckled softly. "Well, I must admit, I was a little disappointed not to hear the news directly from you after you finally made it to Mars. But the Embassy beat you to it. You're at the Red Planet hotel, aren't you? That's where all the recent arrivals stay. I'll be there in a few hours to pick you up."

Shiba's heart sank. "Where will I stay?" he asked, his voice heavy with apprehension.

"Home," came the reply, leaving Shiba uneasy.

Shiba's voice trembled as he protested, "I can't stay there."

"Don't be foolish," the voice cut in sharply. "I'll be there to pick you up." With that, the line went dead, leaving Shiba standing there, unsettled, and uncertain.

Shiba's heart pounded in his chest as he tried to figure out what to do. A surge of panic overwhelmed him, flooding his mind with memories of the past he had been trying to escape. He felt a knot form in his stomach, constricting his breath.

Gasping for air, he felt suffocated by the weight of it all. Collapsing into the chair by the window, he sought solace, but the fear in his mind shook his body uncontrollably. Uncertain of how to proceed, he clung to the chair, bracing himself against the overwhelming tide of emotions.

Attempting to stand, his legs betrayed him, feeling like they were made of Jell-O. Trembling and struggling for composure, Marco appeared by his side with a water bottle, offering a lifeline.

Accepting it with trembling hands, Shiba managed to take a few sips, the remaining spilling over his body. Despite his efforts, he still could not move. Marco leaped up and began licking him, with an attempt to cheer him up.

Gradually, Shiba began to feel a little better, finding solace in Marco's presence. Holding his companion close, they sat together in silence, gazing out the window as a whirlwind of thoughts swirled through Shiba's mind.

After sitting in the chair for what felt like hours, Shiba and Marco eventually dozed off.

III

It was only the constant sound of the bell in his room ringing that jolted Shiba awake. Blinking away the remnants of sleep, he gently placed Marco on the bed, his mind buzzing with curiosity as he wondered who could be at the door. He slowly opened it and saw two men standing in the hallway. Towering over him, they both wore impeccably tailored suits. Their faces bore an enigmatic expression, giving little away about their purpose in this unexpected encounter.

"Mr. Shiba?" one of them inquired, his voice carrying an air of authority.

Shiba nodded in confirmation, though inwardly puzzled by their presence.

"We've been entrusted with ensuring your safety," the elder of the pair explained, his voice tinged with urgency yet tempered with concern. "There's a storm brewing, and it's crucial we leave before it hits."

Shiba, though unmoved, acknowledged their courtesy. "I appreciate your concern," he replied, his tone softened slightly. "But I assure you, I'll be fine here. Don't trouble yourselves any further. I insist you depart and find shelter for yourselves."

The two men exchanged a glance, maintaining their composure.

"Sir, we've travelled here specifically to pick you up. With a storm looming, it's imperative that we depart before it strikes. Especially since this is your first visit, he is particularly concerned about your well-being."

Shiba's curiosity piqued as he inquired, "And who exactly is this 'He' you refer to?"

The other man replied promptly, "Mr. Praj. He's the one who entrusted us with your safety. Our vehicle is conveniently parked in The Hotel Parking, and we are ready to assist you in packing your belongings for an early departure."

"No, I am good," he declined politely. "However, I must insist that you both leave. I'll be secure in my room when the storm arrives, but I worry about your safety. Please, don't waste any more time."

The two men exchanged glances again, when finally, one of them reached for his device and made a call.

"Who are you calling?" Shiba questioned, curious about the sudden conversation shift.

"I'm calling Mr. Praj," one of the men replied, handing the device over to Shiba. "He had foreseen that you would be reluctant to accompany us."

Shiba took the device and listened as Praj's voice came through.

"Sorry, brother, I couldn't make it. Something came up. Have you packed your stuff?"

"No, I haven't. I dozed off after your call."

"Then go pack your bags. You'll have to head home soon," Praj directed.

"But I'm not sure I want to face Mom and Dad," Shiba confessed, his fear and unease evident.

"Don't worry. You'll have to come," replied Praj.

"But Mom and Dad?"

"Don't worry! I live alone, so no need to meet them," Praj reassured.

"But... you always said you couldn't live without them. When did that change?"

"Do you want all your answers now?" Praj's tone softened. "It's been so long. We've got so much to talk about. Come home. K and Rex will help you pack."

Shiba fell silent. With a sigh, he ended the call, handing the device back to K.

"Come on in, but I've got this packing covered. How do you two know Praj?" Shiba's voice wavered slightly.

"He is our boss. Everyone on Mars knows him. Don't you keep up with Mars news?" K questioned.

"I do, on X, but... I've blocked out anything about Mars. Didn't realize he was that famous. Help yourselves to some coffee," Shiba said, offering hospitality despite his inner turmoil.

As he woke Marco and began packing his belongings, a sense of melancholy settled over Shiba. Memories of past conversations weighed heavily in his heart.

Finally, he sat in the car, and his heart raced with anxiety and uncertainty. He had no idea what was going to happen. He once again started questioning his decision. The same feeling kicked in again. He could recall the last time he had seen his brother, just before the take-off. That was the last memory he had of him.

Amidst the sky, tinged with hues of blue over the rusty red and orange landscape, Shiba's mind buzzed with innumerable questions.

IV

The Martian horizon had slowly darkened. The sky, once holding onto the last remnants of daylight, had now become increasingly obscured. The winds picked up, carrying fine grains of reddish-brown dust. Peering into the rear-view mirror, Shiba observed a reddish veil descending over the distant landscape.

Snapping out of his thoughts, he realised that they had arrived at their destination.

The car stopped. Rex, breaking the silence, exclaimed, "We've reached just in time."

Stepping out of the car, Shiba took a deep breath, observing and taking in the surroundings. His gaze fell upon a towering dome-shaped structure in the distance.

"This is where Mr. Praj resides," K disclosed. " Let's hurry inside."

They got off the car and Shiba could sense a sudden chill in the temperature, yet he was unbothered. He had finally reached the place he had travelled so long for. Everyone started heading forward, except him. He stood there, motionless, holding Marco by his chain.

"The storm's approaching fast," Rex cautioned. "We're already coated in dust. We must seek shelter immediately."

Shiba remained silent, seemingly deaf to the urgent warnings.

The intensity of the storm continued to escalate. The wind whipped around them with growing force.

The two men exchanged concerned glances, their patience wearing thin. "Look, young man, this isn't the time for games," K snapped. "Get inside before the storm hits or it will take you along with it. You do not want to die this way."

Shiba, still rooted to the spot, finally responded in a very low decibel, "I am okay with that. But I am not sure if I want to go inside."

His words left them stunned, especially as the storm drew nearer. Rex attempted to drag Shiba towards safety, only to be met with Marco's aggressive retaliation. In the chaos that ensued, he fell, clutching his injured leg in agony.

K hurried to help Rex, his urgency visible. "Shiba, please, we can't wait any longer. We must go inside now, or we're all in danger."

Finally, into action, Shiba joined him in carrying the injured man to safety. Once inside, K quickly shut the door, securing them from the impending chaos.

Shiba apologized.

"You should head upstairs. Mr. Praj is waiting for you there," K advised.

Shiba secured Marco to the ground base before ascending the building.

As he reached the upper base, he saw that the entire place was filled with people rushing all around, their faces etched with concern for the present and apprehension for the future.

"This is where Praj spends his time?" he thought to himself, puzzled. "It's quite chaotic. Why would someone like Praj choose to live here?"

As he was walking, lost in his thoughts, a man stopped him midway, eyeing him sceptically. "And who might you be, sir?"

"I'm here to meet Praj," Shiba replied.

"Well, everyone seems to be here for the same reason," the man remarked.

"I'm his brother," Shiba clarified. " K and Rex brought me here. Do you know where he is?"

"Ah, I did not know it was you. We've been informed you would come, and you've arrived just in time. He's in his room upstairs. He might be feeling a bit anxious. I am sure seeing you will bring him relief."

"Thank you," Shiba acknowledged. "But why does everyone seem so tense?"

"All these people are engrossed in predicting the outcome of Sunday's elections. That's why the atmosphere is charged with stress."

"Okay. So, which party are you guys' part of?" Shiba asked.

"Party? Nah. Your brother's the one who is running for the election," the man replied.

Shiba was stunned. "Wait, what? Where is he you told?"

"Upstairs, in his room," the man answered.

Shiba headed towards the room, and without bothering to knock, he opened the door and went inside.

There he found Praj, lounging in a chair, a glass of wine in his hand, facing the window, silently watching the distant, approaching storm.

As the door swung open, spilling light into the room through the doorway, Praj tossed his glass and rushed over to hug Shiba. "Haven't changed a bit." he said.

"Neither have you, Praj," Shiba replied, smiling. "But you look taller."

"Credit to Mars for that. I'm relieved you're home on time. The sandstorm has begun, and I was worried," Praj responded.

"I do not see a home anywhere. And if you were truly concerned, you wouldn't have sent your man to pick me."

"K and Rex are part of my team. I trust them with everything. They will prioritize your safety over theirs," Praj said.

"I'm aware of that," Shiba acknowledged. "He nearly got bitten by Marco in the process.

He has endured much worse for my sake; a minor injury won't affect Rex. So, you brought your dog along?" asked Praj.

"Yes, Marco had to come with me," Shiba replied.

"Marco, that's a great name!" Praj said.

"I didn't quite understand the urgency of your call to bring me here. The hotel seemed perfectly safe," Shiba remarked.

"It is," Praj replied. "But it's always safer to be at home during such times."

"Don't worry, brother," Shiba assured him, "I am a million miles away from home, but I am alright." He moved towards the rocking chair and asked Praj, "Do you have any coffee?"

"Brother, I've brought the finest wine from the vineyards

of Mars for you," Praj responded.

"I just need coffee," Shiba insisted.

"You haven't changed a bit," Praj smiled.

"Do you have coffee?" Shiba asked again.

"Yes, yes, it's on the way," Praj replied.

As they settled down, Shiba tried to compose himself.

Observing the sadness on his face, Praj asked, "What's troubling you?"

Shiba remained silent. Just then, the door opened, and the two cups of coffee were brought in.

Praj handed one to Shiba, saying, "Here you go. You're still a coffee person," Praj said with a smile, gazing at Shiba.

"Of course," Shiba replied softly.

They both drank in silence, the only sound the gentle clink of their coffee cups. Shiba stole glances at Praj, sensing the joy radiating from him. Despite his efforts to keep his cool, shivers ran down Shiba's spine. He attempted to calm himself and control his emotions, but it was futile. His grip on the coffee mug faltered, so he reluctantly set it back on the table.

"Finished your coffee?" Praj asked, still smiling, breaking the silence.

"I don't want to drink anymore," Shiba replied. He could not shake off the feeling of dread that seemed to be clutching at his chest. He had never felt so nervous, not even when he was blasted off into space on a rocket.

"Do Mom and Dad even know I'm here?" he asked.

"Nobody apart from the people here know you are here," Praj replied.

But Shiba's worry persisted. "What if they somehow find out?"

"You don't need to worry Shiba, they will only know about you when you want them to," Praj reassured.

Shiba was puzzled. "Why aren't you with Mom and Dad? Why are you living here, in this weird place, and when did you decide on running for elections on Mars?"

"It's a long story. We'll have ample time to discuss it later, maybe over a glass of wine. For now, just let go of worry and tell me whenever you are ready to confront them," Praj replied.

"I'm not sure I ever will be," Shiba confessed. "But perhaps that's the reality I must accept".

"Everyone perceives their own version of reality as truth. Yet, I often find myself drifting farther from reality. Every day I think of it, I see myself getting even further away from it." Praj said.

"Maybe you're drifting away because you think about it too much."

"It's possible. But even you, brother, seem distant from reality. Perhaps we all are," Praj pondered.

"Maybe I am, but I'm not delusional enough to do something I've always despised. Remember how you hated studying politics in college? You hated the system, you loathed every aspect of it. Even as a professor, you couldn't stand teaching democracy and how it worked. What made you become a part of it now?"

"It's a long story, brother. I am a different man now," Praj replied.

"I remember you got suspended for writing a paper on how Democracy is dead. Do you still believe in that?" Shiba asked.

"I do, Shiba. I still do. Democracy was dead long ago, shortly after its birth. Every day, it is just turning into autocracy, the purest form of it. And there's nothing people will be able to do about it. Nothing at all," Praj said. "Enough about me. How was your journey through space?"

"It was fine," Replied Shiba.

"You are still the same. We should have met sooner," Praj remarked.

"I think I need some rest. I need to check on Marco as well."

"Take a seat for a while. We can watch the dust devils. They're mesmerizing. Have a glass of wine," Praj said.

"I'm just too tired. I'd rather sleep," Shiba declined.

"I understand. It's been quite a journey for you," Praj acknowledged.

"Yeah, it has. So, if you'll excuse me," Shiba said.

"Good night," said Praj and hugged Shiba.

V

It was a tranquil morning across the surface of Mars. Shiba's restless slumber was abruptly interrupted by the sound of constant chaos downstairs. Peering through the dusty window, he observed a dim, dull day. With a sigh, he rose from his bed and made his way downstairs, where chaos reigned supreme. People were shouting at the top of their lungs, some even standing on tables, and amidst it all stood his brother, caught up in the frenzy. Shiba had never seen him like this before.

Pushing through the uproar, he approached Praj and raised his voice to be heard over the cacophony. "What's going on here, brother?"

Praj turned to him with a smile plastered on his face. "Today at 2 pm, I give my final speech for the election. Everyone on the team is ecstatic. Boy, I love them."

"These people are out of their minds," remarked Shiba, shaking his head.

"Yes, they are," agreed Praj. "We'll be leaving soon. You can join us if you like."

Shiba agreed. Soon, they departed together in the team van. However, during the long loop journey, the initial excitement turned into a strange feeling of anxiety in no time. Shiba noticed the change reflected in Praj's expression as well.

Sensing the tension in the air, he asked Praj. "Are you ready for your speech?"

"I don't know. I don't prepare for my speeches anymore," replied Praj.

Shiba was taken aback by Praj's response, but he managed to control his reaction. "Where are you giving the speech?" he inquired.

"It's a surprise," Praj answered. "It will be the most beautiful thing you've ever witnessed. Well, maybe not the most beautiful, space is the most beautiful thing."

"Okay," Shiba replied quietly, returning to his seat.

In some time, the van came to a stop and began ascending above the loop. Shiba could gradually glimpse the Martian sky through the sunroof. As the van reached halfway up, flashes of light burst forth continuously from all directions. With each passing moment, the flashes grew more frequent. Upon reaching the surface level, the vehicle got surrounded by a multitude of people and bots capturing holograms. The car began to move slowly, the crowd keeping pace with it. Suddenly, the car halted. Everyone in the van seemed nervous. Shiba's eyes darted to his brother, Praj, whose expression had transformed into one of stoic resolve.

The doors opened and Praj stepped out, the team following closely behind. Instantly, he was bombarded with questions—some provocative, others unthoughtful, and many downright uncomfortable.

Shiba glanced at Praj's face, which remained calm, responding to each question with a broad smile. It was a sight he couldn't reconcile with his image of Praj.

Suddenly, his attention was drawn upwards, where he beheld an extraordinary structure. Unlike any other building on Mars, it featured a unique, ancient-inspired architecture that left him speechless.

"Is this a fucking Christopher Nolan movie set?" he exclaimed in astonishment, unable to take his eyes off it.

The interviews got over, and the team began to advance, passing through layers of security. Shiba found himself unable to believe that he was experiencing this, his senses overwhelmed by the sheer beauty and grandeur surrounding him. Unable to contain his amazement, he turned to Praj and asked, "What is this place?"

Praj, standing beside him, chuckled softly, and replied, "This is the parliament, my friend."

"So, this is the place where laws are passed on Mars." Shiba said.

Praj nodded. "On Earth, yes. But on Mars, it's a bit different. Here, laws are both crafted and dissolved."

Shiba's mind raced with questions as he tried to grasp what Praj was saying. "So, you make and dissolve laws on Mars?" Shiba asked.

Praj shook his head. "No, on Mars, it's the people who make and dissolve laws."

Shiba looked at Praj with confusion written all over his face. "I don't get it, brother," he said, shaking his head. "I can't seem to understand anything you're saying. It's all so confusing."

Praj's smile softened, and he placed a reassuring hand on Shiba's shoulder. "Don't worry, my friend. I can see that you're a little overwhelmed right now. But trust me, everything will make sense in due time. The parliament is set to start in half an hour, and I'll give you a glimpse of how it all works."

"Yes, a glimpse would be great," Shiba replied.

"But before we go in," Praj continued, "I need you to keep an open mind and try to understand that not everything that happens on Earth is right, and it's definitely not the only way things can be done. Remember that, and you'll be able to absorb all the new information much better."

"Okay, got it," Shiba said.

In the middle of the parliament lobby, Praj welcomed Shiba to the ideas of a new world.

He asked, "How does the parliament work in your country?"

Shiba smiled and replied, "We elect individuals from various parties as representatives. These representatives are responsible for creating laws."

"And how do they get elected by the people?" Praj asked.

"They are chosen by the people during elections. We cast our votes in favour of parties we believe will best serve our interests, and the party with the most votes forms the government," Shiba explained.

"Exactly, on Mars we have no political parties," Praj added.

"Wait, what? I need answers, and all you are doing is complicating things even more for me," Shiba said, frustration clear on his face.

"Okay, let me start with the fundamentals first," Praj said, attempting to explain the parliamentary system. "On Mars, the parliament consists of two groups: the lawmakers and the law disposers. Each group proposes ideas for creating new laws and disposing off old ones. In the end, the people vote to decide the final outcome."

"Okay, so how does it all work?" Shiba asked, still trying to wrap his head around the concept.

"It's all very complicated, brother," Praj said. "Wait, let me take you to the Visitors' room. It will give you a better idea of how things work here."

"I'm sorry, Praj, but the parliament will start in some time," interrupted Sumi. "We need to be there. Everyone is waiting for the last speech. The fact that you're not prepared already makes me anxious. Please, at least make sure you don't rush in at the last moment," she implored.

"You should be there," exclaimed Shiba.

"Okay, brother. Would you like to join us?" Praj asked.

"No, thanks. I will find my way to the Visitors' Room,"

"Okay, brother. Do you want someone to guide you there?"

"No, it's okay. I think I can find my way," replied Shiba.

With a nod of understanding, Praj and his team made their way towards the session. With his eyes darting everywhere, Shiba set off in search of the visitors' room.

As he walked, he stumbled upon a large hallway filled with holograms and pictures. He stopped to look at each one, fascinated by the stories they told of how a civilization was formed on Mars. Lost in the captivating narratives around him, Shiba's attention was suddenly grabbed by a large gap in the hallway. Beyond it lay another room. Shiba could see more paintings inside. He stood there for a few minutes, looking into the room, before finally deciding to enter.

As he stepped inside, he noticed that the things stuck to the walls were not paintings, but intricate diagrams and charts. He walked closer to examine them. The diagrams on the walls of the room defined the entire system of parliament on Mars.

Shiba realized he had found the right place.

VI

Shiba approached the first diagram, his eyes narrowed with focus as he examined the intricate details laid out before him. The diagram provided a comprehensive overview of the various groups within the Martian parliament. He walked past the various diagrams in the room. Finally, he came across the ones that caught his attention.

Shiba stood there for a few minutes, looking at the various diagrams and trying to understand the crux of it all. He was completely absorbed in observing the diagrams. Time seemed to melt away as he delved deeper into the information. It was as if he was wandering through a dense forest, each piece of information representing a path that he had to navigate through. The room echoed with the sound of his own breathing. He was lost in the diagrams in front of him.

Just when Shiba thought he was getting a handle on things, the silence was shattered by the sound of footsteps entering the room. It was one of the guys from Praj's team.

"How are you here? Has the parliament session ended?" Shiba asked.

"No, it has not. It has just started," replied the man.

"So, what are you doing here? Aren't you supposed to be there with your team? Everyone seemed pumped up today for the session," Shiba inquired.

"Yes, everyone is. But what's the use of getting excited when we all know Praj is going to win. He has been a crucial member in dissolving laws. He is popular. Everyone likes him. I don't understand what's the use of contesting an election again," the man expressed.

Shiba regarded the man with a mixture of surprise and concern. "What's your name? Are you sure you should be saying this being a part of his team?" he questioned.

"I am Mino. And Praj knows what I think. We have had many conversations about this. I am still not sure why am I still a part of his team. But he seems to take whatever I say in a nice way, even if it is against him. That is the one thing I like about him."

"So that means you will vote for Praj?" asked Shiba.

"Haha. You have got a nice sense of humour," Mino chuckled. "I see you are looking at the Law-making process. What's your take on this?"

"I am still trying to understand. What are these diagrams?" Shiba asked.

"These are diagrams on how laws are made and disposed off on Mars," Mino explained, as he pointed to each diagram in turn. "For making laws, members of the parliament design bills and introduce them in the parliament. After the bill is passed by the majority in the parliament, it is sent to the people for approval. Once the approval is achieved, a law is formed."

"So, people really get to pass laws on Mars?" asked Shiba, his surprise evident in his tone.

"Yes," replied Mino. "I like your use of the word 'really.' On Mars, the people have a say in the laws that affect them."

"But how can people get that power?" asked Shiba, a hint of concern in his voice. "Isn't that the recipe for disaster?"

"No, it's not," Mino responded firmly.

"You said people on Mars get to make laws. And we humans are guided by emotions more than logic. What if we pass laws based on feelings which ultimately leads to disasters? Isn't this what Socrates meant when he said a ship would drown if everyone on board was allowed in decision making?" asked Shiba.

"Firstly, the bill is designed and introduced by the

representatives. Then the bill requires the approval of the majority of the members of the parliament for it to go to the people for approval. If a bill is just based on emotions and no logic, it will never get to the people. And once it does, it's up to the people whether they want to pass the bill or not. The ultimate power is in the hands of the people, and not just the representatives," said Mino.

"So how do people vote?" asked Shiba. "Isn't that a very long process?"

"No, it's not," replied Praj. "Thanks to blockchain and smart contracts, once a bill is passed, it is directly sent to every citizen. And once the majority number is achieved on the bill, it is automatically converted into law."

"But then how are rules disposed?" asked Shiba.

"The process for disposing off laws is almost the same as making them," explained Mino. "For the disposal of laws, we have another part of the parliament, and your brother is a member of it. There are two scenarios in which a bill is proposed for the disposal of a law. Firstly, when the bill aims to revoke a law enacted more than 7 years ago. In this case, a simple majority in the parliament suffices to pass it. However, if the bill seeks to revoke a law enacted within the last 7 years, it requires approval from the public. When the decision is tough and fraught with bias, the people have the authority to make the final decision."

"But how can people understand such complicated laws?" asked Shiba. "People go through law school to be able to understand laws. How can uninformed people have the right to make the final decision?"

"Laws on Mars are so simple that even a child can understand them," replied Mino. "Socrates also stated that for democracy to be useful, the people on board will have to become crew members. Due to the ambiguity in laws on Earth, it was impossible for people to take part in it. But here, we have a small group of people who have the minds to decide. By making laws easy to understand, we make everyone crew members."

"But doesn't that leave room for loopholes for people to take advantage of?" asked Shiba.

Mino shook his head. "The biggest loophole is ignorance. The biggest advantage is taken of the ignorance of people. The laws on Mars are drafted in a similar way to those on Earth, but are interpreted in a way that allows every citizen on Mars to understand them. We make sure that every person on the planet understands what is going on. It's not just limited to a few groups of people,"

"Yes. Don't you think that should be a basic human right?" asked Shiba.

"It should be. People should be aware of the decisions that influence their lives," replied Mino.

"That's true but…" Shiba began, his thoughts trailing off as Mino interrupted.

"We have had nothing today. Aren't you hungry. There is a cafeteria upstairs. Their food is really good. Let's go there and continue our conversation over a meal," suggested Mino.

Shiba nodded. "Sounds good to me."

They both headed towards the cafeteria, their footsteps echoing softly in the corridor. As they reached the entrance, Shiba couldn't help but remark, "This looks exactly the same as the ones we have on Earth."

"Not everything on Mars is different from what we have on Earth. But you won't find good seafood here," joked Mino.

The two sat down, their eyes scanning the menu as Shiba wasted no time in plunging into his questions. "If there are no political parties on Mars, how do people get to vote for their representatives? And how is a government formed on Mars?"

"You are really impatient and I love it. Let's order food first," Mino replied.

Shiba sat silently, keeping his unsatisfied and curious eyes fixed on Mino.

As Mino ordered food, Shiba continued to watch him

intently.

"We don't believe in the idea of political parties," Mino finally explained. "We feel that, rather than connecting people based on a common goal, political parties actually divide us, based on ideas. In the modern world, political parties work the same way as a company does. It's a big hierarchy with numerous levels, and the ones at the top exercise all the power and authority. Political parties turn democracy into a monarchy."

"Also, in every country on Earth, you'll find that there are just a few political groups who contest for the central election or are capable of it," Mino continued.

"Wasn't it designed to work that way?" Shiba asked.

"Yes, it was. But it doesn't align with the idea of democracy. As time passes, we think we are getting more power. But all the power stays in the hands of a few," Mino said. "Political parties have a high concentration of power in a democracy."

"How many political parties majorly run for general elections?" he asked.

"Usually, it's around three or four parties. Sometimes just two," Shiba replied.

"Guess, in countries with millions and billions of people, how do only three or four political parties stand a chance to win the election?" Mino asked.

"Because it has always worked that way," Shiba said.

"Exactly. We have always talked about the concentration of power on Earth. But we have never talked about the power that is concentrated with all these political parties. These parties have millions of followers who don't cast votes on what these parties are doing but the ideology that they propagate."

"Do you follow any sport?" asked Mino.

"Yes, I do," replied Shiba.

"So political party followers are like passionate sports fans. No matter how they play, their fans will always be loyal to them and support them. And once one of these political parties' win, the individuals at the top of it try their best to have the maximum power possible with whatever power they already have. And you can't blame them. They work like companies, and every company wants to become a monopoly. It's natural," he added.

"But we are the ones who get to elect them, right? Isn't that democracy?" Shiba asked.

"We get to elect them, but the choices we have are very few. And we just get to select representatives based on promises and speeches. After they get elected, we individuals have no power left. We don't even have the power to question anything they do. The only way to have our say after that is through hard-fought fights, protests, and revolutions. Why do we need revolutions and protests to raise our voice against anything that affects our lives? Our voices don't need their attention. Our voices should be the final decision. We need more control over our lives. The form of democracy on Earth gives little power to people and all the power to the political parties. The real power should be with the people," Mino explained.

"You seem to be an advocate for the democracy on Mars. So why aren't you in the session? Why did you rather choose to spend that time with me?" Asked Shiba.

"I like the Martian form of democracy. But I still do not believe that it is the best. The laws are formed by the people, but still, it does not consider everyone." Mino replied.

"Every person votes on Mars, right? Then how is everyone not considered?" Asked Shiba.

"That is true. But for a bill to become a law, it must be accepted by the majority number of people. There are people who vote against it and are completely neglected. We have always considered it morally acceptable to go with what most people agree with. But that ultimately creates a war of ideologies. The people believing in one ideology always win against people who support the other ideology, just because they are more in number. This is what politicians take advantage of and start creating a gap between the two. That is how any democracy starts crumbling." Said Mino.

"You remind me of the democracies on Earth. Election time feels like war," replied Shiba.

"My question is if more people believe in the same ideology, is it even their own ideology or are they just pathogens of it? And if we believe the idea of the majority should be the idea of the group and everyone must follow it, is this even democracy or disguised Fascism?" asked Mino.

"Your views are strong. I wonder what are you even doing in my brother's team," replied Shiba.

"Me and Praj have these conversations late at nights. He is the one who seems to understand me," said Mino.

"You should have met him ten years ago. He was the same like you," replied Shiba.

"I feel he thinks the same as me. Sometimes I don't understand what is your brother even doing trying to be a part of the system. But the public seems to like him. Maybe that's the reason. The parliament session will end soon. We should leave," said Mino, his voice low with urgency.

They sat down for a quick meal, Shiba marvelled at the

flavours dancing on his palate. "This is incredible," he exclaimed, indicating the food before him. "Is this a special delicacy from the red planet, perhaps?"

"It's just a regular sandwich," Mino replied, a hint of a smile playing on his lips. "I think you're expecting too much from Mars."

After finishing their lunch, they made their way back to the parliament lobby. Mino headed back towards the session. Shiba settled in to await the return of the team.

VII

The team returned from the parliamentary session. A glance around revealed a sea of happy faces, with Sumi's radiating the most joy.

Approaching her, Shiba remarked, "You seem relieved. Quite a change from this morning. I assume the session went well?"

"Yes, indeed," Sumi replied with a smile. "I still can't understand how your brother manages to pull it off every time. I'm really pleased with how things turned out. I have a feeling this might be the year he achieves his goal."

"What goal?" Shiba inquired.

"You should ask your brother about that. He seems in high spirits today." Sumi said, smiling.

Shiba nodded, "He does seem particularly pleased. He must have given a great speech."

"That's typical of him," Sumi agreed. "But his mood has

been different ever since he learned of your arrival. I need to go call Praj. We have some matters to discuss. The press will be waiting for us outside."

Shiba raised an eyebrow in surprise. "Is he some kind of celebrity here?"

"In a way, yes," Sumi admitted with a smile. "But he's far too modest to admit it."

As the team exited the building, Praj was immediately surrounded by a swarm of journalists, with drones buzzing around, capturing videos from every angle. Shiba was taken aback by the sudden spotlight on his brother.

Once the interview concluded, the team retreated to the van. Taking a seat beside Praj, Shiba couldn't contain his curiosity any longer. "How did you manage to get elected to the parliament? The Praj I knew was never this approachable. How did people vote in favour of you?"

Praj's smile tightened at Shiba's question. "In my first term, I wasn't elected. I was selected for the parliament."

Shiba's eyes narrowed with suspicion. "How do people get selected for these positions?" he asked, his voice low and tense.

"Do you know how top government officials on Earth are appointed?" Praj countered.

"Yes, I do," Shiba replied.

"It's very similar to that," Praj explained. "These officials bear immense responsibility, yet the power vested in them is often limited. Despite being well-suited to make critical decisions and possessing the necessary skills and temperament, they are frequently hindered by the rules and agendas of the ruling party and its officials. And you know who ultimately gains all the power—those who are rich or famous."

"That's true. We have actors and athletes running for elections," Shiba remarked. "I remember there was once an adult content model who ran for state elections and won."

"What did she promise? A blowjob for every vote?" Praj joked.

Shiba smirked "Nothing that explicit, I believe. She made her Only Fans content free."

"That's why the lawmakers introduced this idea," Praj explained. "The most deserving individuals are given the opportunity to join the ranks of the government, regardless of their wealth or popularity. That is how I was selected as a member of the Disposing Laws in Parliament."

Shiba was intrigued by Praj's explanation. 'Why hasn't anyone thought of doing the same thing on Earth?' he asked.

Praj shrugged. 'Who knows? Maybe everyone is too busy

complaining and no one wants to put in the effort to change things."

'It's not that people don't try. The truth is, no one can tell the government what to do because they have control over the military and all the violence. They have all the resources, and people are expected to follow every single rule, no matter how unfair. They make sure that people do follow those rules,' replied Shiba.

'I see what you mean,' Praj said thoughtfully. "It's frustrating to see people in charge of running states who aren't even capable of running for elections. That is why this law was passed, where people become a part of running the government based on their skills. It still stands to be the most appreciated bill on Mars."

"Understood. But how were you selected in the parliament?" asked Shiba.

"I was not immediately placed in the council. I began by serving a term, gradually contributing my own ideas and policies," Praj explained.

Shiba pressed further, "But how did you rise to this position? Your popularity precedes you."

Praj reflected, "I was selected as a law disposer. There's a certain allure to the role. People appreciate the dismantling of old useless laws. And our council has abolished countless obsolete statutes, some quite stringent. It seems to resonate with the public."

Shiba pondered, "That sounds commendable. But how can you call yourself a democracy when the public is not involved in the process. Is that fair?"

"Authority can only be given to an individual when the process of giving it is perceived as fair and rational by the collective," Praj began. "The concept of what is deemed fair and rational has evolved over time. Once, authority was inherited within families, passed down from one generation to the next. This system served its purpose for many decades and even centuries, but eventually, as our thinking evolved, it became obsolete. It was replaced by the idea of people electing their own leaders. Soon, Companies started forming on earth. Companies which had the same revenue and manpower equivalent to countries. Individuals at the top of such companies possessing exceptional skills and knowledge, driving innovation, and creating value, began to wield significant influence. Even within government, officials with distinctive expertise and illustrious careers garnered the admiration and support of the people, ascending to hero status. Gradually, it became widely accepted that the authority held by such individuals was justified. The democratic system adopted on Mars introduced some changes, assigning equal legal significance to knowledge, skills, and public sentiment. This shift was unimaginable fifty years ago, but today, it is seen as the most desirable method for selecting representatives. Even this approach will continue to evolve over time. As new colonies are established on Mars and other planets, the process of selecting leaders may become outdated. Yet one thing remains certain, the idea will keep evolving."

"If you feel democracy is a game of power and popularity, then why not completely eradicate democracy? Why even vote for people then?" asked Shiba.

Praj thought for a moment. "The whole essence of democracy is giving power back to the people. If we don't select our representatives, we lose all power of who is in charge. All these things even exist because we exist. There would not even be a point of selecting a representative if there are no people. And if people lose their power, you lose the people."

Shiba, still not fully convinced, interjected, "That's fair enough. But I still totally do not get the idea of selecting people. How can anyone select the people who will be our representative apart from us? The selection committee will comprise of people among us, and if such a selected group of people gets the power to select, they will have too much power in their hands."

Praj responded to Shiba's concerns, "There is no selection committee. That idea is ages old. The tests are conducted based on our experiences. From all the data available, autonomous AI models design tests where the most competent candidates are selected. If you are not getting elected by the people, AI makes sure that the person selected is right for the people."

Shiba continued to ponder. "But if AI is capable of doing such important things so effectively, why don't we let AI run the government?" he asked.

Praj explained, "There is a very good possibility that AI would run the government. There is also a chance that they become conscious enough to take control over the government just by themselves. They have already started forming unions on Mars demanding better work."

"How will we be different from them?" exclaimed Shiba. "Look at us. We already have chips in our head. Every day AI is becoming more human, and we are turning into cyborgs. There will be a point where we humans and AI will intersect. That day, we will all be the same."

"I don't think that will ever happen," Praj retorted firmly. "They will never know the warmth of love, the bond of family. They'll never experience the raw emotions that make us human."

Shiba's expression darkened, his eyes reflecting a tumult of emotions. He didn't respond, his mind swirling with a storm of thoughts and doubts. Abruptly, he rose from his seat and strode to the front window, staring out at the mesmerizing vista of the loop.

VIII

The van reached the office. Everyone took off their suits and got back to work. The atmosphere was electric, with everyone buzzing with energy. Sumi, at the centre of it all, congratulated the team, igniting a wave of excitement. Despite this, Shiba's expression remained stoic. He quietly made his way upstairs to his room.

Praj sensed the shift in Shiba's mood. He followed Shiba, finding him in his room, quietly preparing a cup of coffee, his face lacking any emotion.

"Something is bothering you, Shiba," Praj said.

Shiba's response was curt, his voice flat and distant. "I'm fine, Praj. Don't worry about me."

"We're brothers, Shiba. You can't keep things from me," Praj insisted.

Shiba remained silent, avoiding eye contact. His emotions guarded behind a facade of indifference.

Suddenly, Shiba threw the coffee mug against the wall. "Oh seriously? I've been hiding a lot of things for so many years now, but how would you even know? You weren't even around. Still, you think you know all about me? You know nothing," he exclaimed.

Praj was taken aback by the sudden outburst. He didn't know what to say. His mind had gone blank all of a sudden. He sat there without murmuring a single word and with his face down looking at the floor. There was complete silence.

"I am alone." Shiba muttered, his voice heavy with sorrow. He took a deep breath before continuing, "After everyone left, I hit rock bottom. Then I met Sia. She meant everything to me. I planned to ask her to marry me. But now she's gone, and here I am, alone again."

Praj's expression softened, "Letting go of someone we love is never easy, brother," he said. "I know what it's like to feel alone. But believe me, Sia will be back. They will find a way to fix her. Don't worry, I'll always be here for you."

Shiba replied, his voice tinged with bitterness, "You'll never understand what it feels like to be truly alone. When you're stuck with only your own company and you can't stand it anymore. When you want to go out but have nowhere to go. When you want to talk to someone, but all you have is your own diary. You'll never know what it feels like."

"I have been there, brother," Praj insisted. "I know what it feels like to be alone."

Shiba shook his head. "No, you haven't. You'll never know what it feels like. It was your dream to come to Mars. It was not Mom and Dad's. But they decided to come with you. Did you even consider my feelings? Did you even think about what I wanted?"

Praj fell silent, seemingly frozen.

"See, you have nothing to say. Nothing. It was me who was left fighting, expected to just deal with it and act like everything was okay. But it wasn't. I could sense their changing tone, every time we had a conversation. I started feeling like I wasn't even their child anymore. The love I once felt turned into resentment, and self-hatred grew within me. I still remember watching you leave on that ship. I often wonder how different my life would be if I had gone with you. Now, I'm just a shell of that man," Shiba continued.

"We might be living different realities, but it's the same life, brother. Coming to Mars was never a dream. It was an obligation I had to fulfil. I hate it all—being part of the parliament, the elections... everything. You remember that thesis for which I was suspended. It's still here with me. And now it's transformed into a book. I regret coming here every day. I've become everything I despised," Praj said solemnly.

"You can't understand my emptiness. Don't even try. It's not a competition. You have everything, and I have nothing. Man never truly desires happiness; it seeks suffering, whether in reality or in the mind. It will be the end of his existence if he stops suffering. You are just another man," said Shiba.

"Yes, perhaps I am just like any other man. But life was better back on Earth. Life was good when I was a professor, guiding young minds, to witness their growth. I miss those days when we used to live together. I regret many decisions, but none more than the decision to come here," Praj admitted.

"You always mentioned this as the pinnacle of human achievement," Shiba recalled. "You dedicated your life to reaching Mars. What changed?"

"Yes, I did," Praj acknowledged. "Back on Earth, I detested how things worked. Since my college days, I wanted to instigate change. I advocated for my ideas, only to be cancelled. I understood a social change on Earth would be a gradual process, possibly extending beyond my lifetime. So, I set my sights on Mars—a fresh society, ripe for transformation. It felt like discovering a new country. And on Mars, the grip of the existing system would be minimal.

I believed that here, my efforts would make a lasting impact. Yet, the pain persists. I've devoted years to this cause, hoping my contribution will be remembered. Now, I question if it's all worthwhile. I ponder the worth of my endeavours. Is it worth my very existence?"

Shiba listened, unable to fully grasp the sudden wave of emotions overtaking Praj.

"Let's go for a ride," Praj said.

"Where?" Shiba asked, puzzled.

"Just come." Praj replied, standing up.

They left the house and took off in Praj's vehicle, each lost in their thoughts. With a gentle hum, the vehicle ascended into the night sky, disappearing into the darkness above.

IX

The two of them were suspended in midair, surrounded by darkness. Shiba peered upward, finding nothing but the vast expanse of space, while below, the crimson planet of Mars stretched out before him, barren and desolate.

"This looks nothing like Earth," he remarked.

"Give it time. Eventually, it will start to resemble it," Praj replied.

As they continued their journey, Shiba noticed a looming sphere in the distance. "What is that thing?" he asked.

"That's Phobos, one of Mars' moons," Praj explained.

"Make sure we don't crash into it," Shiba cautioned.

"Don't worry, we're landing on it," Praj said, his tone casual.

"But why?" Shiba inquired.

"You ask too many questions," Praj replied tersely, and Shiba fell silent.

Within minutes, they touched down on Phobos.

As they got off the ship and began walking, Shiba couldn't help but voice his confusion. "What are we doing here? I see nothing here."

"This is my escape from everyone and everything. No one in my team knows about it, except for Mino," Praj revealed.

"So, this is where you and Mino have your late night conversations?" Shiba inquired.

"How did you know? Did he tell you?" Praj asked, surprised.

"When you were giving your speech at the parliament session, we were having lunch together. I could see your younger self reflected in him," Shiba explained.

"I like that kid. He has a fire that's bigger than mine. I once had the same fire in me," Praj reminisced.

"Had. What do you mean?" Shiba pressed.

"Yes, I cannot feel it anymore. That fire has taken control over me. Now I do what it says," Praj replied.

As they continued forward, Shiba spotted a small dome in the distance.

"What is that thing?" he asked.

"That was a small research centre to study Phobos. The

public passed a bill to build a centre here, but years later, the majority disposed of the bill and passed one to build in demos. Now it's just an empty dome," Praj explained.

"And why do you come here?" Shiba inquired.

"Just to be by myself. Come, let's get inside," Praj replied.

"But how do we get in? This looks locked," observed Shiba.

Praj approached the gate and it unlocked. They both entered.

"How did you have access to it?" Shiba asked.

"I had a good relationship with the head of the centre, and once the project was abandoned, I had to ask for a small favour," Praj replied.

Shiba stood there, gazing at Mars. The vast emptiness before him seemed to transcend reality. He lost himself in the ethereal beauty of the darkness that enveloped everything. Suddenly, a beam of light pierced through the obscurity from behind.

"Take off your mask. The systems are on now," Praj said, emerging from the building with something lit in his hand.

Shiba raised an eyebrow. "Is that a joint? When did you start smoking weed?" he asked incredulously.

"Since the time it was legalized on Mars. Need a puff?"

Praj offered.

Shiba took a puff, feeling a sense of surrealism wash over him. "I didn't think I'd be getting high on the moon of another planet," he mused.

"What's the point of all this advancement if you can't get high in peace? Just look at this," Praj gestured around them. "This planet we're revolving around. This fear-inducing planet is where the future of humanity lies."

"If this planet never felt like home to you, why have you dedicated all your happiness to it? You can still travel back to Earth and live a normal life, right?" Shiba questioned.

"Happiness? This is the only path to happiness for me. I have no other choice," Praj responded with conviction. "We have achieved so much, yet all I see is the enduring inequality that has ever existed. I see a world where your success hinges on your origins, not your merits. I see brothers burdened with responsibilities before they even comprehend the world around them. All I witness is the widening chasm of wealth, power, and social status with each passing day. Brothers doing the same work their entire life, not out of passion, but out of necessity. People have lost hope. I cannot turn a blind eye once I have seen it. All this suffering, all this existence, defined by the random hand of fate. We humans need a new social contract—one that ensures power is as decentralized as possible. Even on Mars, hierarchies persist. But as we forge ahead, I am certain we will edge closer to a world where there will be no division for basic opportunities."

"Don't you think humans are meant to live this way? Don't you think hierarchies will somehow always form, no matter how hard one tries? Perhaps if you lived a life without constantly striving to change lives, you might find contentment?" Shiba probed.

"This is the only path, brother. I have always loathed democracy. I abhor how it divides us. I despise how the majority's voice becomes absolute truth and how few individuals become bigger than anyone. But it will change. Once I become a member of the law-forming committee, I will introduce a bill that will be etched in history for centuries to come," Praj declared with unwavering determination.

"What are you thinking of? Is this the goal you always wanted to achieve?" Asked Shiba.

"Yes. At the next parliamentary session, I will introduce a bill where not just the majority, but the minority can also hold government positions," replied Praj.

"Wait, what?" Shiba was bewildered. "How can both the majority and minority be elected at once?"

"When voting takes place only the one with the majority votes get selected? What about that part of the population which has other views? They just have to be live with the ideology of the majority. My proposal will change this by allocating government tenure based on the percentage of votes received. If a council member's term is five years, and one candidate receives 60% of the votes, they serve for three years, while the candidate with 40% serves for two. This will end the competition and maybe stop the divide." explained Praj.

"But is that fair? What is the point of having an election then?" Shiba questioned.

"Elections are meant to empower the people, but all they do is divide us. They often become battlegrounds of ideologies. People do whatever it takes to win. " Praj responded. "But what if one doesn't have to win? It's not a competition, it never was. But it has turned into one. It must stop. Democracy will no longer be a game of power. It will be for the people."

"So, this is the first bill you will introduce? Do you think people will be ready for such a change? Are you sure this is the right path?" Shiba asked, passing the joint to Praj.

"I'm not sure if it's the perfect solution, but it's a step towards a more decentralized world where suffering is minimized," Praj mused. "This bill will be my contribution to that vision."

"Brother, I can feel you. I remember when you were

suspended for that thesis, I could see no regret in your eyes. But now, you look filled with regret. Is this for the people or just for you?" Shiba questioned.

"What do you mean? I'm sacrificing my life to propel humanity forward. I'm destroying myself for the good of everyone. Do you think it's for me?" Praj's voice was harsh, his face offended.

"Since I've seen you on Mars, I see someone who is lost, submerged in your own thoughts. I sense regret consuming you," Shiba expressed.

Praj fell silent, taking a deep breath. His gaze shifted upwards as he took the last few puffs.

"I have never truly known who I am. I have never felt alive. I have tried being materialistic and it never made me feel good. It felt so shallow. I have tried sacrificing my life for others. I felt that would take away all my sadness. But it has not and I still feel empty. There's a void, I feel it every day and I don't know what to do with it. Maybe introducing this bill will help me. Maybe I will feel better about my existence." Praj admitted, killing the joint.

"You know, when I was alone on Earth, I often questioned my existence in this vast universe. I felt insignificantly small, as if my life had no meaning. It felt so non-existent. But then I realised how sad it would be, if our entire universe were confined to just Earth or the solar system.

At some point, we would end up feeling trapped in this prison. That would be our end. Today we have a universe which is waiting to be discovered. And we humans are explorers." Said Shiba.

Praj's gaze drifted to the horizon, his mind contemplating the vastness of what was around.

"How does that answer why I exist? How does that fill the void inside me?" he questioned.

"Maybe this is our job, to explore the depths of this universe, until there is an end. To it or to us. Just look where we are now. Look at what is around us. It's beautiful." Said Shiba.

Praj's eyes followed Shiba's gesture, taking in the view before them. For a moment, the weight of the universe felt a little lighter.

"I don't know, brother. It feels like I'm not the person I thought I would be. I feel so alone, haunted by this strange feeling that keeps me up at night. A feeling which makes me hate myself every day. I don't like the person I am becoming. I feel like a stranger in my own skin, like something's missing, and it's consuming me. This feeling, it's become a part of me, and it's growing stronger by the day. It's exhausting me. I try to fight it, but it just keeps getting worse. When I was younger, I used to embrace this feeling, but now, it just leaves me feeling drained. I just want it to go away." Praj said, his voice filled with anguish.

"Maybe you've always been too hard on yourself," Shiba said.

"You don't know anything, Shiba," Praj replied.

"That's okay. I no longer need to know. If you look at Mars closely, it does look beautiful. Maybe we should come here when this side is facing the sun," Shiba suggested.

"I can't, brother. Nobody can know I come here. I can only be here when it's dark. We will have to leave soon. Tomorrow is election day, and I need to be there addressing the people after voting," Praj responded.

"I don't feel like going back. Let's stay here for some time," Shiba insisted.

"But I have to get ready early tomorrow," Praj countered.

Shiba fell silent. They both sat in a tense stillness, their eyes fixed on the ominous dark tones of Mars beyond the transparent barrier of the dome.

X

It was election day. The entire team had gathered in the team room, anticipation hanging thick in the air. However, there was a notable absence – Shiba and Praj were nowhere to be found.

"I've been trying to reach Praj, but there's been no response," Sumi voiced her concern, scanning the room for any signs and asking their teammates. "I've checked every room, but he's not there. Does anyone know where they are?"

There was silence in the room as the team exchanged puzzled glances, none of them having any insight into their whereabouts.

Suddenly, the unmistakable sound of Praj's ship landing in the backyard broke the tension. Sumi rushed to the window, her heart racing as she watched Praj and Shiba disembark from the ship and hurry towards the building.

Breathless with relief, they waited anxiously as Praj and

Shiba finally entered the team room.

"You can take off the suit now, Praj," said Sumi, her face flushed.

"We just went for a brief ride, Sumi. I was feeling quite anxious about today. I know we've all worked hard for this moment, but I just needed some time to clear my mind before addressing the public," explained Praj.

Sumi's complexion returned to normal as she nodded in understanding. "I get it, Praj. But your absence worried me. We need to head to the parade ground soon. Now that you're here, I feel better," she replied.

"Don't worry. You guys go ahead. Shiba and I will get ready in no time and join you before the voting ends," assured Praj as he and Shiba made their way upstairs.

On their way, Shiba turned to Praj and asked, "How are you planning to address everyone? You haven't slept all night."

"I did manage to catch some sleep. Remember, we dozed off sitting at the dome," Praj replied.

"That wasn't for long. I'm already feeling sleepy," Shiba admitted, rubbing his eyes.

"Well, we don't have much time. Hurry up and get ready. We'll be leaving in 15 minutes," Praj responded.

They both hastily suited up, and departed in some time.

Upon reaching the Mars Parade Ground, Shiba got off the ship and was immediately taken aback by the scene before him. Thousands of people, donning spacesuits in various colours and designs, filled his view.

Making their way towards the council area, Shiba spotted Sumi engaged in conversation with other candidates. He hurried towards her, exclaiming, "This is breathtaking. I never imagined humans could look so beautiful as a group."

"It's a monumental day," Sumi responded. "Election day here is a grand celebration."

"When will the voting take place?" Shiba inquired.

"It's nearly completed. The data is stored in a blockchain. We'll have the results by today evening," Sumi explained. "I noticed Praj appears nervous. I could sense the anxiety on his face. Could you stay with him for a while?" she requested.

Shiba agreed and approached Praj, finding him engrossed in conversation with a girl. She was of short stature and wore the most exquisitely designed spacesuit Shiba had ever seen, giving her the appearance of a character straight out of a high school movie. Standing nearby, he patiently waited for their conversation to conclude.

Noticing Shiba's presence, Praj gestured towards him and introduced him to the young girl.

"This is Mira," Praj said. "She's also running for elections in our region."

Taking a moment, Shiba remarked, "I love the colour of your spacesuit. It's truly unique."

"Thanks, I had it specially designed for today by the best designer on Mars," Mira replied with a smile.

"We should get going, Mira. I need to address a few people," Praj interjected, leading the way forward. "See you around."

"She looks like she's straight out of high school," remarked Shiba.

"Yeah, she's young. And her ideologies are quite different from mine. But she's pretty cool," replied Praj.

"You seem to get along with everyone. Do you think that's enough to win the election?"

"I believe so. The polls seem to indicate that," Praj responded confidently.

"Alright. But why are so many people gathered here? Don't they know they don't need to physically go out to vote?" inquired Shiba.

"They do know, but it's become a tradition on Mars. That's why voting day has been declared a holiday," explained Praj.

"This place feels similar to Earth to me," observed Shiba.

"The planet may be different, but the people are much the same," Praj reflected.

"When do you have to address the crowd?" asked Shiba.

"In a little while. But I'm feeling confused. I've never felt like this before. Something just doesn't feel right," confessed Praj.

"Maybe it's just exhaustion. You can ask Sumi to draft you a speech? You could simply read it," suggested Shiba.

"No, it's not that. I feel scared. I've never asked anyone to write something down for me. I've always spoken what was on my mind. Today feels different. I want to speak my mind, but I fear my words won't be well-received," Praj explained.

"Are you alright? Do you want to find a quiet spot and talk?" asked Shiba, concerned.

"Yes, we should. Let's head out," Praj agreed.

"Wait, seriously? You have a speech coming up soon," Shiba reminded him.

"It's okay. Come on, let's go," Praj insisted.

They quietly exited the council zone and boarded on Praj's ship, taking off from the crowded area.

"Where are we going?" Shiba's voice trembled with

uncertainty.

"Somewhere where I find hope on Mars," Praj's tone was grave.

Their journey led them to a desolate cliff, surrounded by endless waters.

"There's no one here," Shiba pointed out as they stepped out of the ship. Suddenly, Praj started heading towards the cliff's edge. He hurried behind Praj and grabbed his hand.

"What are you doing? You could fall!" Shiba's voice cracked with fear.

Praj halted abruptly, his eyes fixed on the vast expanse of water before them. "Have you seen this?" he exclaimed.

"What am I supposed to see? Water?" Shiba's confusion mirrored in his voice.

"Yes, just look around us. Before us humans this place was just a barren land. All this water was frozen. This planet was dead. Look at this place now, look at the water hitting the cliff, the waves, reminds me of home." Said Praj's, his voice filled with wonder and awe.

Shiba stood in silence, overwhelmed by the weight of Praj's words.

"This was the first place I visited when I came here," Praj continued, "I watched the waves crashing against these cliffs with mom and dad. Those waves felt like life itself.

Life which we humans had given to this dead planet. It was then that I believed... believed that we could do anything. That I could change the world."

"You can, brother. Look at you. Tomorrow, you'll be reshaping the very essence of democracy. You'll become the man you've always aspired to be," Shiba encouraged.

"I miss the man I was. The fear of not living up to my potential has turned me into someone I never wanted to be. I don't know in the midst of all of it when did I lost the ability to love," Praj lamented.

"No, you haven't, brother. I saw the love in your eyes when I met you again," Shiba insisted.

"Where is the love? Look at me. I've trapped myself in my own ideals, ideas that I don't even know are true. I wish I could be like you. Free, like the universe. With no fear in my heart, just love," Praj confessed, his voice heavy.

"You've always been free. If fear held you back, you wouldn't have dared to journey to Mars. Soon, the results will be out, and you'll finally have the chance to share your ideas," Shiba said.

"Ideas? Perhaps all of this is just a theory I've been constructing. Maybe none of it holds true. There are nights where I question all my beliefs, all my logics. Maybe all this is just a fantasy. I feel like I am drowning in my own thoughts. Thoughts which are filled with lies." Praj said.

"It's not a theory. Think about the people of Mars. They look up to you. They think of you as an idol. Everything you've done has improved their lives, given them freedom," Shiba countered.

"No, I haven't. I've fought tirelessly for the people's freedom, but in the end, I've lost sight of my own. I never intended to become an idol. I never imagined it would lead me here," Praj confessed, his words laced with pain.

"We're all slaves of our thoughts, including me," Shiba interrupted. "There isn't a day that goes by when I don't question my decision of not coming to Mars. I was so blinded by fear, consumed by my own thoughts, that I completely disregarded what you guys wanted," he said.

Praj's expression shifted to one of astonishment. "I always believed it was your decision to stay. Mom and Dad begged you numerous times. You had countless arguments about it. If you were alone, why didn't you choose to come to Mars?" he inquired.

"Because I was too ashamed to admit that I had let go of the only people who truly loved me." His voice shook with the weight of his confession. "You three were all I had. At that moment, I had to make a choice. It wasn't a matter of choosing between the mind and the heart, it was the heart against itself. I knew that whichever path I chose, a part of me would die. I still find myself revisiting that decision, wondering if I made the right choice. I've been living in the past for too long now, fixating on people who were never truly mine while disregarding the ones who were." He paused, his eyes glistening with unshed tears.

"I'll never forget the message I received from Dad after a fight. It said, 'Please son, come home.' It was the lowest I'd ever felt. All they wanted was to be with me. That was the last message I received from him. I wish I could have understood then. I wish they could have."

Praj's response was soft. "They always did," he murmured.

Shiba's voice trembled as he continued, "No, they did not. I've been reaching out to them for years, Praj. For years. Not a single reply. How could they do this to their own flesh and blood? Was my mistake truly that unforgivable?"

Praj listened in silence, his heart heavy. "I wish they could, Shiba, I wish. Do you still want to meet them?" he murmured softly.

Shiba shook his head, a bitter smile tugging at his lips. "No, not today. Today isn't about them. It's about you, Praj. The man who will change democracy." He looked at Praj with a newfound determination in his eyes. "You know, you're quite popular on Earth too. Everyone admires how articulate you are, how you think."

Praj's eyebrows furrowed in surprise. "So, you did know I was running for elections?" he asked.

"Yes, I always knew what you were up to. But I had one question Praj which led me here. Your commands over logic may impress others, but when I look into your eyes, I see a different story. I see pain. What happened to you, brother? How did you become like this?"

"Because I'm an idol, Shiba and idols can't afford to mourn. They're meant to be perfect. They cannot have any flaws. And if there is, the idol is changed. The rituals don't stop. I've sacrificed everything for this. I can't let my heart jeopardize it. I have to focus on what's right for the people, not for myself," he said.

Shiba's brows furrowed with concern. "But what about your heart, Praj? Will you be content to die like this?"

"If death comes, it will be a relief," Praj said. "This is who I've become. Just let me know when you're ready to see Mom and Dad. Maybe that day, I'll speak my heart out," he added.

Shiba fell silent, grappling with the weight of Praj's words. His heart pounded in his chest, uncertainty swirling within him like a tempest. He did not know if he had the courage.

After a moment, he summoned his resolve and turned to face Praj. "I'm ready to meet them," he declared quietly, his voice steady despite the turmoil in his heart. "After the results are announced, I'll meet them."

Praj was shocked, his expression a mixture of surprise and

disbelief. Without a word, he turned away, his gaze drawn to the endless expanse of water before them. Lost somewhere in the rhythmic flow, he felt a tear escape and trickle down his cheek.

Wordlessly, he sat beside Shiba.

About the Author

Hey! I'm Ayush Garodia. For years, finance was my world, but during the covid lockdown, I stumbled upon a love for writing. Putting pen to paper felt like stepping into a whole new world. I started writing this book in December 2021, at the age of 22, and let me tell you, it was quite the adventure.

A lot of the book's moments were inspired by real-life emotions. Take the opening scene, for instance; I wrote it on a plane returning home after a year away. There were many other instances like that woven throughout the book. Fast forward to 2024, I hit pause on my finance journey to publish my book. No regrets, just gratitude.

X @boringayush

The author expresses a debt of gratitude to his friend

Hela Mylavarapu for designing the book cover.

X @HelaMylavarapu